Soccer

mc Marshall Cavendish
Benchmark
New York

This edition first published in 2010 in North America by Marshall Cavendish Benchmark

Marshall Cavendish Benchmark
99 White Plains Road
Tarrytown, NY 10591
www.marshallcavendish.us

Published in 2009 by Evans Publishing Ltd, 2A Portman Mansions, Chiltern St, London W1U 6NR

Editor: Nicola Edwards
Designer: D.R. Ink
All photographs by Wishlist except for page 6 © 2008 Getty Images; page 7 © 2008 Getty Images; page 8 © 2008 AFP; page 12 © 2008 AFP; page 13© 2004 Manchester United; pages 18/19 © 2006 AFP; page 24 © Bongarts/Getty Images; page 26 © 2006 Getty Images; page 27 © 2007 Getty Images

The author and publisher would like to thank Luke Chiltern, Callum Goodridge, Natasha Seeney, Harvey O'Shea, Jake Cox, Jordan Clayton, Phil Lines (Coach), and Brackley Town Football Club for their help in making this book.

Library of Congress Cataloging-in-Publication Data

Gifford, Clive.
 Soccer/by Clive Gifford.
    p. cm. — (Tell me about sports)
 Includes index.
 Summary: "An introduction to socccer, including techniques, rules, and the training regimen of professional athletes in the sport"—Provided by publisher.
 ISBN 978-0-7614-4460-2
 1. Soccer—Juvenile literature. I. Title.
 GV943.25.G5492 2009
 796.334--dc22

                              2008049024

Marshall Cavendish Editor: Megan Comerford

Printed in China.
135642

Contents

Soccer

▲

Cristiano Ronaldo scores a goal for Manchester United against Chelsea in the 2008 Champions League Final.

Soccer is an amazing, exciting team sport. A full game of soccer (also called football) has eleven players per side, but games with fewer players are played, too. The aim is to kick or head the soccer ball into the other team's net to score a goal. The team that scores the most goals wins the game!

Players line up in rows of **defenders**, **midfielders**, and attackers. This is called a team's formation. Players can control and move the ball with any part of their body except their hands and arms. Goalkeepers (one on each side) are the only players who can handle the ball, providing they stay inside their penalty area.

A full game is made up of two halves, each 45 minutes long with a 15-minute halftime break in the middle. In

some competitions, if the score is tied, overtime is played.

Soccer is a very popular sport. The number of women's professional teams is growing. Star players like the United States' Kristine Lilly and Germany's Birgit Prinz are famous.

Soccer is played by millions and watched by many millions more. At the highest level, top players amaze fans with their spectacular skills. But people can enjoy themselves by playing a casual game in the park.

Soccer Fans

- Over 100 million people worldwide watched the final game in the 2008 Champions League between Manchester United and Chelsea.

- According to FIFA, the organization that runs world soccer, 715.1 million people watched the 2006 World Cup final between Italy and France.

- One fan in The Netherlands was so passionate about his country's team that during the 2004 European Championships, he painted his entire house the color of The Netherlands team stripe—bright orange!

▼ Millions of fans all over the world watch soccer. They are passionate about their teams. The sport is fast and full of action and drama.

Scoring Goals

Goals win soccer matches. Teams with talented scorers often have an advantage over teams with less-skilled scorers. One of the things that makes soccer so exciting is that anyone on a team can score a goal. When you are playing in a match, you need to react quickly and shoot for the goal accurately.

To score a goal the whole ball must cross the goal line in between the goalposts. When you play, remember that your shot may hit a **defender** or bounce off the post. This may give you another chance to score.

▼ Chelsea star Frank Lampard has sent his shot out of the reach of the goalkeeper and the defender, Rio Ferdinand (*left*).

How you hit the ball at the goal will vary. If the ball is high in the air, you can head it toward the goal. If you are close to the goal, you can use a side-foot shot. This is a firm pass of the ball into the goal.

A **volley** is when you hit the ball in midair. It is a powerful shot but can be hard to control. You need to keep your body balanced and not lean back as you kick through the ball.

▲
The attacker (in red) has kicked the ball toward the goal. If the goalkeeper doesn't make a save, a goal will be scored.

▶
The attacker (*left*) reaches the ball before the goalkeeper and heads it toward goal.

Super Scorers ⚽⚽⚽⚽⚽

● The Germany player Miroslav Klose scored 16 World Cup goals for Germany. In 2014, he beat the previous record held by Ronaldo of Brazil.

● The great Brazilian player Pelé scored a staggering 1,088 goals for the Brazilian team Santos.

The Field and Gear

A full-size field covers a big area—about 110 yards (100 meters) to 120 yards (110 m) long and between 70 yards (64 m) and 80 yards (70 m) wide.

The edges of the field are marked with sidelines and, at each end, goal lines. A halfway line divides the field in two.

A game starts with one side kicking off from the center spot. None of the other team's players is allowed inside the center circle until the **kickoff** has happened.

The game continues until the ball goes out of play. This is when the whole ball passes over a sideline or goal line. It matters which team touches the ball last. For instance, if the ball goes over your goal line and you touched it last, then the other team will get a **corner kick**.

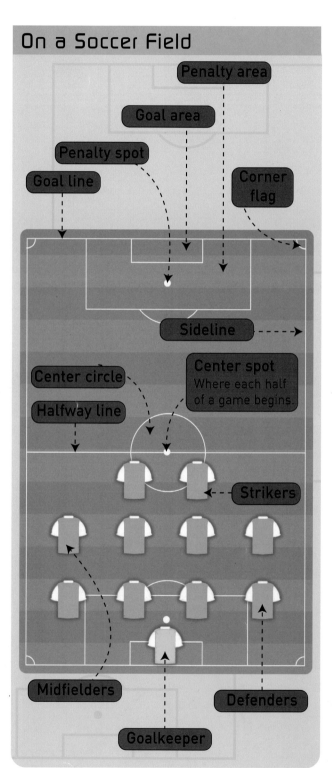

On a Soccer Field

Penalty area

Goal area

Penalty spot

Goal line

Corner flag

Sideline

Center circle

Center spot
Where each half of a game begins.

Halfway line

Strikers

Midfielders

Defenders

Goalkeeper

Putting the Ball Back in Play

Soccer Gear

Soccer clothes are simple—a shirt, shorts, and long socks. The socks cover up strapped-on shinpads that protect your lower legs. Soccer shoes, called cleats, come with studs on the bottoms to help grip the turf. You wear tracksuits to keep warm during training.

When the ball goes out over the sideline, the team that did not touch it last takes a throw-in. Throw the ball over your head with both hands. Both your feet must stay behind the sideline until you release the ball.

This player takes a corner kick. He aims to kick the ball into the other team's penalty area and give a teammate a chance to score a goal.

A goalkeeper takes a **goal kick**. This kick is taken from inside the goal area. It is awarded when the ball rolls out of bounds over the goal line and the goalkeeper's team did not touch it last.

Star Players

▶ Top players such as Deco (*right*) and Ronaldinho (*center*) work very hard on their speed and agility. Here, they sprint and weave in and out of cones on the ground.

Top soccer players are as rich and famous as many film stars. They are professional athletes, which means they are paid to play soccer. They live glamorous lives but they have to work hard, too.

Top players train hard with their team for many hours most days. Training helps improve players' overall fitness so that they can keep running for the entire game. Star midfielders like David Beckham or Michael Ballack may run more than 12,030 yards (11,000 m) in a single match!

Players practice skills such as passing, tackling, heading, and ball control over and over again. They also work with teammates on moves called **set pieces**. These are designed by the team's coach or manager to outwit other teams.

While top soccer players are well rewarded, they do have many responsibilities. They have to eat a healthy diet all the time and prepare for each game and training session carefully.

Terrific Transfers ⚽ ⚽ ⚽ ⚽ ⚽

● Zinedine Zidane is the world's most expensive player. He was transferred in 2001 for over $70.7 million.

● In 1927, Hughie McLenahan was transferred from Stockport to Manchester United. The fee? Three freezers full of ice cream!

Soccer players are often **transferred** between different teams, sometimes for huge sums of money. But if a player does not perform well in matches, he or she may be dropped from the team and struggle to win back his or her place. The same can happen when a player is injured.

▼ Manchester United and England star Wayne Rooney is surrounded by fans as he signs autographs.

ROONEY

Passing

You can use three parts of your foot to pass the ball. Use the inside of your foot for short passes. The top, or instep of your foot (where the shoelaces are), is best for longer, more powerful passes. Use the outside of your foot for short flicks to the side.

You need to aim your pass very well. You want to give your teammates the best possible chance to get the ball. Make sure you are looking to see where they are and in which direction they are heading.

▼ These players are practicing their passing in a small space. The three players in red must try to pass and keep the ball away from the two defenders.

To make a side-foot pass, turn your foot so your toes point outward and swing back and then forward into the ball. Make sure as much of the inside of your foot as possible makes contact with the ball. Your foot follows through in the direction of the pass.

With most passes, your foot should hit the middle of the ball. If you want to hit the ball higher into the air, aim your foot at the bottom half of the ball.

Once you have passed the ball, don't stand still. Get moving so that you can help out your team. Try to move to a place on the field where you can receive a pass.

Passing is very important in soccer. Practice passing with both feet as often as possible. This doesn't have to be boring. You can play fun drills and games where you pass and move around, trying to keep the ball under control.

▼ To make a longer pass, place one foot to the side of the ball and swing your other foot back and then forward with your toes pointing down. Hit the middle of the ball with your instep.

Ball Control

When the ball comes toward you, you must first try to get the ball under control. Aim to keep it near your feet so that you can pass, shoot, or run with it. You can use many parts of your body (except your hands and arms) to control the ball.

Lots of times, the ball will be traveling fast. You can slow it down by relaxing the part of you that connects with the ball just as it arrives. As the ball gets close, move that part of your body backward to cushion the ball.

Heading the Ball

Heading is important in attack and defense. To head a ball, arch your back and then move your head forward so that the middle of your forehead connects with the ball.

Try to keep your eyes open as long as possible. This helps you head the ball accurately.

◄ Heading the ball with the middle of your forehead doesn't hurt. Honest! This player has jumped up to make a header while in the air.

Controlling the Ball

Use the inside of your foot to slow a ball down that's rolling across the ground. Move your foot back just as the ball arrives.

As a high ball falls toward you, raise your leg. As the ball is about to land on the top of your thigh, lower your leg. This will slow the ball down.

You can use your chest to control the ball, as well. Slow the ball down by leaning back as it arrives. The ball should drop in front of you.

Keep It Up!

● Some players practice their ball control by juggling with their feet, head, and chest. Amin Agushi and Bujar Ajeti headed a soccer between them 11,111 times in a row in 2003 in Starnberg, Germany!

● In 1995, Brazilian Milene Dominguez kept a ball up in the air without letting it touch the floor for over nine hours! Four years later, she married Brazilian striker Ronaldo.

Once the ball is under control, you have to decide what to do next. Make sure an opponent doesn't take the ball away from you. Do this by moving around to keep your body between your opponent and the ball.

▼ Move the ball with small nudges of your feet. Try to keep your head up to see players around you.

Attacking

Attacking is about getting players and the ball close enough to the other team's goal to try to score. Sometimes, one player may **dribble** the ball down the field, but mostly it takes great teamwork to attack well.

Players in the attacking team pass the ball around while looking for an opening near the goal. They run to positions where they are not guarded, hoping to receive the ball from a teammate. If you make a run and the ball is not passed to you, don't stop. Try to make another run soon after.

Sometimes, there will be lots of undefended space down the sides of the field. A player can receive the ball

and run into this space before passing the ball into the penalty area with a kick called a **cross**. Crosses can be low to the ground or high, aiming for the head of a teammate.

Dribbling is moving with the ball under close control to avoid defenders. Good dribblers practice their skills for hours. This is so they can control the ball as they turn and swerve to trick and get past defenders. Only dribble when you're not near your own goal since dribbling is risky and you might lose the ball.

Great Goals

● In a 2001 World Cup qualifying game, Australia beat American Samoa 31-0!

● U.S. women's player Mia Hamm holds the national team record for goals. She has scored 158 times.

● In May 2008, LA Galaxy's David Beckham scored a goal from well inside his own half, hitting the ball nearly 20 feet (6 m)!

● A shot hit hard from inside the penalty area can reach speeds of 62 mph (100 km/h). It will take less than a second to cross the goal line.

▼ In this sequence of photos, Brazil's Ronaldo shows his dribbling skills as he fakes out his opponent and gets by him while keeping control of the ball.

Defending

Defending is all about stopping the other team from scoring goals. Good defending stops the other side's attacks and allows your team to regain the ball.

Every player on a soccer team, even the strikers, should try to defend. When your team loses the ball, try to get back into a position between the ball and your goal. This way you are helping to block your opponents' path to the goal.

A defending team often **marks** opponents. This is when a **defender** stands between the goal and an opponent and moves as the opponent moves. The aim is to stop the opponent from receiving a pass.

▼ The players in the striped shirts are marking an opponent each. They aim to stick close to their opponents as they move.

Defending takes teamwork and players must call to each other. Sometimes you can guide an opponent with the ball toward the sideline, away from the goal. A defender with one or two teammates in support may then be able to steal the ball back by making a tackle.

Tackling is when you use your feet to challenge an opponent who has the ball. You must be careful to kick only the ball and not your opponent, otherwise the referee will call a **foul**.

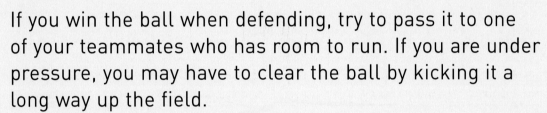

If you win the ball when defending, try to pass it to one of your teammates who has room to run. If you are under pressure, you may have to clear the ball by kicking it a long way up the field.

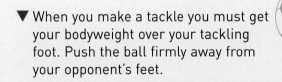

▼ You must work as a team when defending. Here, a defender knows that his teammate is in support behind him so he can move in close to make a tackle.

▼ When you make a tackle you must get your bodyweight over your tackling foot. Push the ball firmly away from your opponent's feet.

Goalkeeping

Goalkeepers are there to stop goals from being scored. Sometimes they make spectacular diving saves. At other times, they have to concentrate hard and organize the team's defense by shouting clear instructions.

Good goalkeepers make many saves look simple. They do this by moving their feet quickly so they can get their body in line with the ball. They can then save the ball with their body behind it for extra safety.

Goalkeepers

- Goalkeeper Rogerio Ceni has scored more than 80 goals for Sao Paulo, his team in Brazil. That's the most goals ever scored by a goalkeeper.

- Italian Gianluigi Buffon was transferred for $50.3 million in 1999. That made him the world's most expensive goalkeeper.

- Until 1912, goalkeepers could handle the ball anywhere in their half of the field. Today's rules only allow them to handle the ball in their own penalty area.

◀ To catch a high ball, spring high into the air and stretch your arms up. Get your hands around the back and sides of the ball.

Sometimes you cannot get both hands on the ball. Then you need to punch the ball out as far and as high as possible. Or use your hands to push the ball around the goalpost.

To make a diving save, push off using the foot nearest the ball. Spring to the side and stretch out your arms to get your hands behind the ball. As you land, try to gather the ball into your chest.

◀ To gather a ball that is rolling toward you, drop to one knee. Get your body behind the ball and scoop it up with both hands into your chest. Wear goalkeeping gloves, which are designed to protect your fingers and give you a good grip.

Soccer Rules . . . OK!

► When a free kick is just outside the penalty area, a team has a great chance to attack and score. The defending team usually makes a wall of players to help protect its goal.

An official called a referee makes sure that players follow the rules, or laws, of the game. Two assistants, who run along the sidelines, help the referee.

Referees start and stop the game using a whistle. They also decide when the ball has gone out of bounds and which team should restart the game.

Referees will stop the game if there is a serious foul. Fouls include tripping or pushing opponents, pulling their shirts, or unfairly stopping them from getting to the ball.

For most fouls, a referee awards a **free kick**. The ball is placed where the foul happened. Players in the team that made the foul have to stand at least 11 yards (10 m) from the ball.

Sometimes a team performs a serious foul in its own penalty area, such as deliberate **handball** (when players try to cheat by touching the ball with their hands or arms). Seeing this, the referee will award a penalty kick to the opposing team. The ball is placed a little under 11 yards (12 m) from the goal. The penalty kicker will try to get the ball past the goalkeeper (there are no other defenders in the way) and into the goal.

▲
You need to stay calm to score on a penalty kick. Some players get nervous and completely miss the goal.

▲
Players have to be careful not to foul their opponents by shoving them or pulling on their shirts.

◀
A referee may warn a player who is making a foul or being rude by showing them a yellow card. For violent play or very serious fouls, the referee shows a red card. Then the player has to get off the field, leaving the team with one less player.

The World of Soccer

In the past, soccer players usually played for a team in their own country. Today, players move all over the world to play for top soccer teams in major competitions.

Soccer teams compete against each other in groups called leagues. The biggest leagues are found in Europe—in countries including Spain (*La Liga*), Germany (*Bundesliga*), Italy (*Serie A*), and England (the Premiership). Other leagues, such as Major League Soccer in the United States and Australia's A-League, are very popular as well.

The best teams in a country may also play against teams from nearby countries. In South America for example, the best teams from each country play against each other in a league called the *Copa Libertadores*.

National teams from each country in a continent play against each other, too. Euro 2008, for instance, featured the best national teams in Europe and was won by Spain. The CONCACAF Gold Cup, won by the

▲
Italy's captain Fabio Cannavaro holds his winning team's 2006 World Cup trophy.

United States in 2007, is the biggest competition in North and Central America.

The most famous competition in soccer is the World Cup, which is held every four years. In this competition, 180 countries compete to be one of the 32 teams taking part in the finals. The women's World Cup also takes place every four years. In 2007, Germany beat Brazil in the final, which was held in China.

Competitions

- The world's smallest league is in the Isles of Scilly in the Atlantic Ocean. Just two teams, the Woolpack Wanderers and the Garrison Gunners, play each other week after week!

- When Spain and Turkey each had a record of 2-2, they had to decide which team would enter the 1954 World Cup by tossing a coin. Turkey won!

- A total of 199,850 fans crammed into Brazil's Maracana Stadium to watch the final of the 1950 World Cup.

▼ Kristine Lilly, wearing number 13, has competed in five women's World Cups for the United States. By 2007 she had played 340 times for her country. This is a world-record number of appearances.

Where Next?

These websites and books will help you to find out more about soccer.

Websites
http://www.fifa.com/worldcup/index.html
The official homepage for the World Cup with news of the qualifying for 2010 and lots of facts and pictures about previous World Cups.

http://www.kidsfirstsoccer.com/
A website with tips on how to plan and coach soccer.

http://www.matchmag.co.uk/
The website of the excellent soccer magazine for younger fans.

http://www.mlsnet.com
The homepage of Major League Soccer (the MLS) in the United States.

http://www.thefa.com/Skills/#Scene_1
Test out your soccer skills online at the Soccer Association's fun website.

Books
Crisfield, Deborah. *The Everything Kids' Soccer Book.* Avon, MA: Adams Media Corporation, 2002.

Hornby, Hugh. *Soccer.* New York: DK Publishing, Inc., 2005.

Soccer Words

corner kick A way of restarting a match. The ball is placed in the corner of the field and kicked into play.

cross A long pass from the sides of the field into the center near the other team's goal.

defenders Players whose main job is to stop the other team from scoring.

dribble When a player moves the ball under close control with his or her feet.

foul An offense that happens when a player breaks one of the rules of soccer.

free kick A restart awarded to one team after a foul by the other team.

goal kick A kick taken in the goal area after the ball has rolled over the goal line.

handball A foul when a player touches the ball with his or her hand or arm.

kickoff The start of the game.

mark When a defender guards an opponent to try to stop him or her from getting the ball.

midfielders Soccer players who play in the middle of the field and who are skilled at both attacking and defending.

set pieces Ways of restarting a match, including corner kicks, free kicks, and throw-ins.

transfer When a player moves from one team to another.

volley When the ball is hit while it is in the air.

Index

Numbers in **bold** refer to pictures.